CIVIL WAR SPIES

BEHIND ENEMY LINES

by Camilla J. Wilson

SCHOLASTIC INC.
New York   Toronto   London   Auckland
Sydney   Mexico City   New Delhi   Hong Kong

Dedicated to my mother,
Carrie Lee Wilson, and to Rod Miller,
my friend and research guru.

ISBN 978-0-545-13002-8

15 14   18/0

Printed in the U.S.A.   40
First printing, October 2010

Contents

Introduction

What was it like to be a spy?

Writing with invisible ink, hiding battle plans in the soles of one's shoes, tucking messages within the folds of pinned-up hair—all were methods used by spies during the American Civil War.

Yet spying was in some ways more dangerous than dodging bullets. A uniformed soldier might survive the dangers of battle. If captured, he would be treated as a prisoner of war.

But the punishment for spying on either side was death, usually by hanging. Despite that risk, thousands of Union and Confederate soldiers served as spies. Many of the most effective spies worked in networks, where they developed a variety of ways to send their messages.

Civilians in both the North and South also risked their lives to spy. Some of the most successful spies were women and African-Americans, both male and female. For example, a white woman who had posed as a man in the Union Army became a spy. She used sodium nitrate to darken her skin and entered Confederate territory as an African-American woman on one occasion and as an African-American man on another.

Allan Pinkerton, who before the war had operated a Chicago detective agency, became chief of intelligence under Major General George B. McClellan of the Union Army. To gain intelligence, Pinkerton used a wide web of connections, including deserters, peddlers, merchants, and prisoners of war. Former slaves and women of both races often provided the best intelligence because they were not as likely to be suspected of spying.

Both sides in the war used the telegraph and coded messages to relay information. The North in particular used manned balloons to observe Confederate positions. The North and South employed flags and torches extensively for signaling. Some African-American spies even developed systems of using laundry to send messages.

Introduction

William Norris in the Confederate Secret Service probed the Washington, D.C., area for information. Eventually, he oversaw an intricate chain of information gathering, using a variety of espionage activities and coordinating dispatches to nations abroad. The Confederate Secret Service became the first "all-source" intelligence network in the U.S.

Spies on both sides of the war displayed great skill and courage. Yet today many of their achievements have been forgotten. This book tells some of their incredible true stories.

Allan Pinkerton

The Detective Who Saved Lincoln's Life

Allan Pinkerton was tough. A barrel maker who had fled his native Scotland, he avoided drowning in a shipwreck off the coast of Nova Scotia. In 1842, he settled in Dundee, Illinois, and began building wooden barrels to make a living. One day Pinkerton learned about a stand of oak trees (good for barrel making) on a nearby deserted island. However, when Pinkerton reached the island, he discovered he wasn't the only one there.

A band of counterfeiters was hiding on the island, busily making fake coins. Pinkerton returned home, found the local sheriff, and offered to take him to the criminals. With Pinkerton's help, the sheriff surprised and arrested the crooks. Just a few years later, Pinkerton became a local deputy sheriff. Eventually, Pinkerton moved to Chicago, where he became a deputy sheriff of Cook County.

Each time Pinkerton changed jobs, he took his skills with him. Being a barrel maker required physical strength, which was a great asset for a deputy sheriff. Serving as a police officer helped Pinkerton learn how the city worked. Pinkerton soon discovered that railway theft was a major criminal activity.

Ever alert to new opportunities, Pinkerton began calling on railroad companies. By 1850, he had started his own business: the Pinkerton National Detective Agency, which specialized in railroad security.

Pinkerton's work as a railroad detective brought him in contact with powerful people, including George McClellan, a railroad executive who would become a Union general in the Civil War. Pinkerton also met Abraham Lincoln, an Illinois attorney representing one of the same railroads.

In the following decade, political and social divisions erupted throughout the U.S., pitting pro- and antislavery groups against one another. By the time Lincoln was elected president of the United States on November 6, 1860, Southern states were threatening to secede, or leave the Union. Soon, South Carolina became the first state to secede, and by February 1861, a total of seven states had seceded. President-elect Lincoln maintained that war could be avoided; however, he wouldn't take office until March. Many of Pinkerton's railroad clients began to worry about how their companies would fare in a war between the North and South.

One of Pinkerton's clients, the Philadelphia, Wilmington, and Baltimore Railroad, engaged him to go to Baltimore, Maryland, to assess the activities of Southern secessionist groups in the city. Bordering Washington, D.C., the federal capital, Maryland considered itself a Southern state. If Maryland and Virginia seceded, Washington would be surrounded by Confederate states. The railroad executives feared that secessionists might cut the rail lines to isolate Washington from the rest of the North. This was a serious risk not only to the railroads but also to the Union.

In Baltimore, Pinkerton sent his undercover agents to spy on the secessionist groups. Soon he discovered a much more disturbing plot than cutting the rail lines: a scheme to assassinate President-elect Lincoln as he passed through Baltimore on his way to his inauguration in Washington.

One of Pinkerton's detectives had infiltrated the

Baltimore group selected to kill Lincoln. This agent revealed the plan to Pinkerton. The assassination was set to occur at the Calvert Street train depot in Baltimore, where the Lincoln train would stop. A crowd of secessionists would gather there well ahead of time so they could fill up the nearby streets and alleys. The chief of the Baltimore police department was involved in the plot. He intended to send a small group of officers to the depot. Once Lincoln stepped off the train to address the crowd, some conspirators would start a commotion nearby. Police officers would dash off to quell the disturbance, leaving Lincoln surrounded by his enemies.

At least eight assassins had drawn ballots to shoot Lincoln. Following the murder, a steamer in nearby Chesapeake Bay would take the escaping assassins to a port in a Southern state. The would-be killers expected to be received as heroes.

Pinkerton had to convince Lincoln not only that his life was in danger, but also that he should take a secret train to Washington. Neither would be easy. The inauguration was scheduled for March 4. Lincoln already was en route to the nation's capital. Along the way, he stopped in major cities to meet supporters and introduce himself to important people. By the time Pinkerton caught up with Lincoln, he already was in Philadelphia, Pennsylvania.

"Up to this time Mr. Lincoln had been kept in entire ignorance of any threatened danger," Pinkerton wrote in his autobiography, *The Spy of the Rebellion*, "and as he listened to the facts that were now presented to him, a shade of sadness fell upon his face."

Despite the alleged dangers, Lincoln insisted on proceeding to Harrisburg, the capital of Pennsylvania, where he had promised to visit the state legislature. Pinkerton stayed up much of the night devising a plan for Lincoln to avoid the crowds in Baltimore.

During the Civil War, important messages routinely were sent from city to city by telegraph. Pinkerton contacted the head of the telegraph company and asked him to "fix" the wires to prevent any communication about the president-elect from passing over the lines so the conspirators wouldn't be tipped off.

Lincoln traveled to Harrisburg the next day, attended the legislature, and met the governor of Pennsylvania. Lincoln was scheduled to attend a reception that night, but Pinkerton came up with a secret plan to sneak him out of town.

A special train waited on a side railroad track in preparation for the trip back to Philadelphia. The horse-drawn carriage that people thought would take Lincoln to the reception instead took him to that train. Pinkerton's orders to the telegraph operators worked perfectly.

"The city was soon entirely isolated from her neighbors," Pinkerton later wrote. "No message could possibly be sent from Harrisburg, and the capital of Pennsylvania was cut off temporarily from the rest of the world."

Kate Warne, the superintendent of Pinkerton's agency, had made special preparations for Lincoln's secret train trip—to bypass Baltimore late at night and go directly to Washington. Warne set up the "rear half of a sleeping-car for the accommodation of her invalid brother," who was none other than Lincoln. The train reached Philadelphia after 10 P.M. There, Lincoln's party took a carriage and switched railroads, entering the sleeping car by the rear door.

"Mrs. Warne came forward, and familiarly greeting the President as her brother, we entered the sleeping-car by the rear door without unnecessary delay, and without any one being aware of the distinguished passenger who had arrived," Pinkerton later wrote.

At every bridge crossing along the way, Pinkerton operatives flashed signals that all was well. The train reached Baltimore around 3:30 A.M., hours before the assassins expected to waylay the president. Still, this was a critical point in the trip. The sleeping car was pulled by horses from the Philadelphia, Wilmington, and Baltimore depot over to the nearby station for Washington. They had to wait two hours before departing.

"During that time, Mr. Lincoln remained quietly in his berth, joking with rare good humor with those around him," Pinkerton said.

As they waited, the group overheard snatches of secessionist chatter and songs outside their train. "'My Maryland' and 'Dixie' appeared to be the favorites," Pinkerton wrote, "and . . . Mr. Lincoln turned quietly and rather sadly to me and said: 'No doubt there will be a great time in Dixie by and by.' How prophetic his words were, the succeeding years too fully proved."

Finally their train departed, and by 6 A.M. they arrived in Washington.

Pinkerton and his detectives had saved the president's life. Yet Lincoln's enemies wasted no time in accusing him of fear and cowardice for "sneaking" into Washington instead of arriving with public fanfare. Political cartoonists drew pictures of Lincoln creeping into the city, and editorials questioned the new president's judgment. Some accused Pinkerton of making up the assassination attempt to gain publicity for his detective agency.

Lincoln's inauguration took place in March 1861.

Allan Pinkerton

In April, Confederate forces attacked Union troops at Fort Sumter, South Carolina. The Civil War had begun. Soon thereafter, Lincoln sent word to Pinkerton to come to Washington. Pinkerton was asked to set up the first U.S. Secret Service. Eleven Southern states had seceded, so it was important for the Union to maintain control of the border states, especially Maryland, as well as Missouri, Kentucky, West Virginia, and Delaware.

After the war ended, Pinkerton returned to Chicago and expanded his private detective agency. Six railroads served as the detective agency's early clients. Now businesses from banks to mines employed the agency. The agency thwarted heists of all types, from a $700,000 robbery of the Adams Express Company in 1866 to major railroad thefts. Pinkerton detectives took on the Western gangs as well, capturing the Reno brothers, who specialized in robbing trains, and tracking the notorious Jesse James gang.

By the 1880s, Pinkerton was rich and famous. He published several books, writing about the role he played in thwarting the 1861 assassination attempt and helping to win the war and abolish slavery.

"Very often, as I sit in the twilight, my mind reverts back to those stirring scenes of by-gone days," he wrote in the conclusion of *The Spy of the Rebellion*.

The Detective Who Saved Lincoln's Life

"More than all do I rejoice in the freedom it brought to nearly half a million of people, who, prior to that time, had been held in inhuman bondage. . . . The war is over, the rebellion has been crushed. . . . The flag of the Union floats from every port in the United States, the slave is free, the South is recovering from the ravages of war, and the stories of those stirring times seem now like the legends of an olden time."

The Ultimate Sacrifice

Lying in a thicket of leaves, twenty-one-year-old Confederate scout Sam Davis savored the thought of breakfast. Life was beginning to look up. Here he was, lying in the brush like a big old bear, waiting for someone to bring his food. Being a courier certainly had benefits, such as not having regular soldier's duty.

But it could also get you killed.

Sam had outfoxed death more than once. He had served under Confederate general Robert E. Lee in Virginia, had been wounded at the Battle of Shiloh, and wounded again at Perryville, Kentucky. Then Sam lucked out. General B. F. Cheatham had called for volunteers to serve as couriers (special messengers) and scouts in his intelligence group, known as Coleman's Scouts. Davis volunteered.

Technically, the scouts were not spies. They wore Confederate uniforms and were officially part of the Confederate Army. However, they gathered information on federal troops for Confederate general Braxton Bragg, the chief commander in their region. Whether recognized as a spy or not, Sam knew the dangers if captured by Yankee soldiers. Suddenly, he heard horses, and two young women approached.

"We found him up, looking as bright as if he'd slept all night," wrote Mary Kate Patterson years later in an 1896 edition of *Confederate Veteran* magazine, "and oh, he did enjoy his good warm breakfast."

Many local citizens assisted Coleman's Scouts, as did relatives and girlfriends. Sam's half brother, John Davis, had helped found the Scouts, and Mary Kate Patterson was his girlfriend. On this morning, she brought a cousin, Robbie Woodruff, along as well. Not only did they bring breakfast and news of what was happening in Smyrna, Tennessee, Sam's hometown, but they came to assist the Scouts, too. Sam had a wish list ready for the young women: half a dozen newspapers from Nashville, the nearby capital of Tennessee; toothbrushes; soap; and blank writing journals. He expected to deliver those hard-to-find items to General Braxton Bragg's headquarters in several days, along with important documents he would pick up later.

Scouting had its benefits. Sam had been assigned to his old neighborhood. He knew many of the people he encountered in his information gathering; he could catch up with friends, relatives, and former teachers and classmates.

Sometimes Sam could even visit his parents' home, but he had to slip in in the middle of the night. The Union had its spies in Tennessee, too, so one couldn't be too careful. Sam was especially close to his mother, Jane Simmons Davis, a woman known for her kindness. She had nine children and was always looking for ways to help them. She was the second wife of Charles Lewis Davis, one of the wealthiest men in Rutherford County. Sam tried hard to please his father, a man with a strong sense of honor who attempted to pass on his values to his son.

Mary Kate and Robbie spent a pleasant day with Sam. Later, the women went home to prepare to go to Nashville and purchase the items Sam needed.

The thicket was becoming comfortable to Sam. But when the women returned with the requested supplies, he loaded his horse and placed the items in waterproof saddlebags. After darkness fell, he rode south toward Pulaski. He had a meeting to attend.

The Ultimate Sacrifice

Sam's new role as a scout was somewhat similar to the games he had played as a child. Southern men from well-to-do families learned to be good horseback riders. Spying was almost like a sport, but the dangers were real. A misplaced message or a discovered document could cost someone his life. Even so, many of Sam's friends and relatives left messages in hollow logs and under stones, just as they had done when they were children.

Coleman's Scouts consisted of forty to forty-five members secretly supported by relatives and friends who hid them, purchased their supplies, or aided them in other ways. Orders to members of the group carried the signature "E. Coleman." However, the head of the group was not actually named Coleman. He was Captain Henry Shaw, a former teacher at Tennessee's Western Military Institute. Shaw had created a new identity, disguising himself as a bearded herb doctor who pretended to traipse through the woods looking for medicinal plants. In reality, "Dr. E. Coleman," gathered information about Union troop movements. He pretended to limp and passed through military lines, both Union and Confederate, at will.

Soldiers in Coleman's Scouts carried Confederate passes inscribed, "E. Coleman, commanding Scouts, by order of General Bragg." Only a few of the Scouts knew Coleman's real identity, and the federals never suspected. Sometimes Shaw met his couriers personally, particularly if he had especially important information. On November 18, 1863, Shaw set up a meeting with Sam and two other couriers, W. J. Moore and Joshua Brown. Sam reportedly spent the night at or near the house of a contact named Bob English. Houston English, a slave belonging to Bob English, had apparently stolen a document from a senior Union commander, Grenville M. Dodge. English had snatched the document from Dodge's desk while he was having dinner. Suspecting that a spy was on his staff, Dodge would stop at nothing to identify and destroy the spy network. He could not imagine that a slave would steal the message.

General Dodge served an important role in the Union Army—his troops guarded vital railroad lines. Dodge was also charged with intelligence, the gathering of information about the enemy. The theft of his own documents infuriated him.

Just as spies used "creative" methods to carry out their orders, General Dodge decided to try a new tactic as well. He commanded the 7th Kansas Cavalry, known as the Jayhawkers, to deal with the troublesome Scouts.

Wars often create a need for special military units. Before the war, the Jayhawkers had been a pro-Union militia that opposed slavery in Kansas. They were known for stealing horses and using violence to gain information. Their unit included a marksman who later would be known as Buffalo Bill. The Jayhawkers were now directed to kill or capture Coleman's Scouts.

The three Scouts were ordered to travel different routes to General Bragg's headquarters. But only one of them—Sam Davis—was to carry documents. To evade capture, "E. Coleman" instructed Sam to take a lengthier route toward Chattanooga and to cross the Tennessee River near Pulaski, then to circle around General Bragg's army before entering Bragg's camp.

November weather in Tennessee can vary between sunny days and freezing drizzle. Riding in an icy wind, Sam pulled his heavy coat close. How he wanted to turn his horse north toward his hometown. His parents' house offered warmth, hot food, and his mother's touch.

Davis recalled his last visit home. He had waited until night to visit. He didn't want his younger brothers and sisters to see him. They unintentionally might reveal they'd seen him. Many people in the community knew that he might be a courier for Coleman's Scouts. News traveled, and Union troops were everywhere. Sam couldn't be too careful.

The Davis plantation lay on Stewarts Creek outside Smyrna. Their home, a handsome two-story house, stood on a hill above the creek. In the dark, Sam slipped across the yard and glanced into a window to be sure no one was visiting. He saw only his mother and father. Sam gingerly tapped on the windowpane, and his mother quietly opened a side door. She hugged him. His father held out his hand. Sam couldn't stay long. He carried documents and didn't want to endanger his family if he was caught.

Sam's mother hurried to make him a plate of food. His father noticed his boots, which were worn with wear. Charles Davis was a good cobbler, so he set to work repairing them. Sam carried fresh maps of military fortifications around Nashville—they were hidden in the soles of his boots. His father didn't mention the papers as his skilled fingers patched the boots, perhaps because he knew what a danger they posed.

Sam ate and took a last look at his sleeping younger brothers and sisters. He needed to be on his way. A quick hug for his mother and another handshake for his dad—then he slipped out the door. The night was bitterly cold, and his mother noticed that he shook as he went out into the wind.

"Come back in," she gestured. Sam wore only his Confederate uniform, which she had made for him.

The Ultimate Sacrifice

She knew it was not heavy enough to keep out the cold. She fetched a heavy wool coat, the kind worn by Union soldiers. She'd dyed it butternut gray, using shells from a black walnut tree on the farm. Sam thankfully donned the coat and took off. He had many miles to go.

Sam headed toward General Bragg's headquarters. Captain Shaw had instructed him to make a wide circle on his trip and to cross the Tennessee River near Pulaski, where there would be fewer Union soldiers. However, by the time Sam reached Pulaski, the Jayhawkers and other federal units were combing the area. The Jayhawkers had already captured the other two Scouts, Joshua Brown and W. J. Moore. Jayhawkers did not treat captives pleasantly, so the Union troops likely had learned that another member of the Scouts would be passing through the area.

Neither Brown nor Moore carried documents, so the Jayhawkers scoured the countryside for the missing courier, the one with documents. Soon the Jayhawkers closed in on Sam's trail.

There had been good reasons to form a spy network out of a group of former students and teachers. The Civil War created such a patchwork of conflicting loyalties that no one knew for sure on which side many individuals stood. For instance, many African-Americans provided information to Union troops because slaves and former slaves believed the Union Army was more likely to support freedom than the Confederates. Yet Houston English, a slave, had stolen a Union document to help the Confederacy—perhaps because he wished to; perhaps because he was forced.

Just as Houston English's allegiance was unpredictable, so was that of Captain Levi H. Naron, known as Chickasaw, who had lived in Mississippi for twenty-one years as a slave owner. Yet when war came, Naron chose to join the Union, and he, too, had been assigned to catch Coleman's Scouts.

Chickasaw was skilled at hunting and tracking, and he practiced deception like spies did. Chickasaw outfitted his Union troops as Confederate soldiers. When they encountered Sam, riding alone, Chickasaw pretended to conscript him (force him to serve) in the Confederate Army.

This angered Sam. Not only was he already in the Confederate Army, he protested, but he was on "special business" for General Bragg. When Chickasaw's group demanded his weapons, Sam attempted to flee on his horse. One of Chickasaw's men grabbed his bridle. Too late, Sam realized that the men were not fellow Confederates—they were federals!

Chickasaw and his group took Sam to the headquarters of General Dodge. The other two Scouts,

Moore and Brown, were already imprisoned there, along with a strange herbal doctor who limped. The federals sensed that the doctor was odd but suspected no connection to the Scouts.

Federal soldiers searched Sam and his belongings. They discovered the maps under his saddle and other items in his saddlebags. Inside one of his boots, they discovered a letter signed "E. Coleman," describing federal troop strengths and movements. General Dodge attempted to question Davis.

"Davis was brought immediately to me, as his captors knew his importance," Dodge later wrote. "They believed he was an officer, and knew he was also a member of Coleman's command."

Dodge described what happened next: "Davis met me modestly. He was a fine, soldierly looking young man, dressed in a faded federal soldier's coat, one of our army soft hats and top boots. He had a frank, open face, which was inclined to brightness."

Dodge informed Sam that he knew he was a spy. But if Sam revealed who gave him his information, Dodge would give him a horse and safe passage through the lines.

"I discovered that he was a most admirable young fellow, with highest character and strictest integrity," Dodge wrote. "He replied, 'I know, General, I will have to die; but I will not tell where I got the information, and there is no power on earth that can make me tell. You are doing your duty as a soldier, and if I have to die, I shall be doing my duty to God and my country.'"

Sam's father had taught him about duty and honor. Sam did not lie, even though he had been captured by deceptive soldiers disguised as Confederates. General Dodge ordered Sam confined with the other prisoners and placed a secret Union informant in the group. The prisoners didn't talk.

Furious, Dodge ordered Sam brought before him again. If Sam did not reveal who the infamous "Coleman" was, then he would face trial and, if convicted, be hanged. Once again, Sam refused to answer questions.

General Dodge filed two charges against Sam. The first was spying. Sam had been wearing a Union overcoat, implying that he was a Union soldier. Actually, Sam's mother had dyed his overcoat a butternut gray, the color of a Confederate uniform. According to military rules, a captured soldier wearing a uniform was to be treated as a prisoner of war, not as a spy. But that did not deter General Dodge.

The second charge was that Sam was a carrier of "mails, communications, and information" to persons "in arms against the United States government." Sam pleaded innocent to the first charge and guilty to the second, which was not punishable by death.

However, the military court found Sam guilty of both charges and sentenced him to hang the next day, November 27, 1863. Sam had expected to be found guilty but did not expect to hang.

In the prison, Sam's refusal to betray anyone had impressed soldiers on both sides. James Young, chaplain for the 81st Ohio Infantry, the group ordered to perform the hanging, visited Sam in his cell. They spoke about Sam's home and family. They prayed and sang Sam's favorite hymn, "On Jordan's Stormy Banks." Then Sam asked for a pen and paper to write his last letters home.

Pulaski, Giles County, Tenn.
Nov. 26, 1863
Dear Mother,
Oh how painful it is to write to you. I have got to die tomorrow morning — to be hung by the federals. Mother do not grieve for me. I must bid you good bye for ever more — Mother, I do not hate to die. Give my love to all.
Your Dear Son Sam

Mother, tell all the children to be good. I wish I could see all of you once more, but I never never [will] no more.

Mother and Father,
Do not forget me, think of me when I am dead,
but do not grieve for me, it will not do any good.

Father,
You can send after my remains if you want to
do so, they will be at Pulaski, Tennessee. I will
leave some things too with the hotel keeper for you.
Pulaski is in Giles County, south of Columbia.

As dawn broke the next morning, a wagon carrying an empty coffin rumbled up to the tent where Sam and the chaplain had spent the night. A guard detail stood silently as Sam climbed aboard the wagon. In appreciation, Sam gave his overcoat to the chaplain. No one spoke. Soldiers marched in rhythm, a muffled drum rolled, and the mules clipped along—the only sounds as the detail reached the hanging site on Seminary Ridge.

The provost marshal, Captain W. F. Armstrong, looked at Sam and reportedly said, "Sam, I would rather die myself than execute this sentence on you."

Sam replied: "That's all right. You are only doing your duty."

Sam climbed the platform to the gallows. Just as the hangman stepped forward with a white hood,

Chickasaw, the chief of the scouts who had captured Sam, rode up to the scaffold.

Chickasaw called out the general's offer once more—Sam's life for the name of the person who gave him the documents.

"I will not tell," Sam replied. "I would die a thousand deaths before I would betray a friend."

Chickasaw turned away, the hangman placed the noose around his head, and the deed was done.

Approximately a month later, a Davis family neighbor, John C. Kennedy, drove a wagon into Pulaski. Next to Kennedy sat Oscar Davis, Sam's younger brother. The Davis family had sent them to retrieve Sam's body and take it home to the family cemetery.

Kennedy drove to the courthouse in Pulaski to see the provost marshal. Kennedy needed to request passes to be in the area, and he had to ask where the body had been taken.

The provost marshal sternly asked what he wanted. When Kennedy explained that the Davis parents had asked him to bring their son's body home, the officer's face softened. He offered his hand.

"Tell them, for me, that he died the bravest of the brave," the provost marshal said. "An honor to them and with the respect of every man in this command."

The provost marshal provided Kennedy with passes and told him where the body had been buried. When Kennedy made his way back to the wagon, he found Oscar Davis surrounded by federal soldiers, who had suspected why they were there. Some shook their heads and said Sam "ought not to have been hung."

The next day, the two men dug up the body. The white hood still covered his head. They stopped back at the provost marshal's office before leaving. This time, they met the chaplain, who provided them with a few items that Sam had left—a small book and some buttons. He also related the story of Sam's last two days.

By this time, word had spread among the federal troops. As Kennedy and Oscar Davis drove out of Pulaski, federal troops respectfully removed their hats.

Mrs. Davis waited sadly at home. When she heard the clip-clopping of the returning mules, she ran to the window. When she saw the coffin, she fainted.

Davis's mother reburied Sam's body in her garden, where she often worked in the herbs and flowers. That way, she said, she could keep him close by.

Two years after Sam died, members of Coleman's Scouts donated money to the Davis family for a monument in memory of Sam. The inscription read: "He laid down his life for his country. He suffered death on the gibbet rather than betray his friends and his countrymen."

When Sam's parents died, they, too, were buried with their son. Monuments for all three family members still stand on the grounds of the Sam Davis Home, maintained as a Tennessee museum.

In Pulaski, where Sam was hanged, a monument stands in the courthouse square. In Nashville, a statue of Sam Davis stands on the grounds of the state capitol. On the statue's plaque are words spoken by Confederate hero Sam Davis before he was hanged: "The boys will have to fight the battles without me."

African-American Spy

Former slave John Scobell made his way north from Richmond, Virginia, to the Union lines outside Washington, D.C. He had heard that federal troops protected ex-slaves and employed them for building fortifications. Union soldiers directed him to the tent of Allan Pinkerton, the recently hired Chicago detective engaged in setting up the federal Secret Service. Scobell had no way of knowing what a stroke of good fortune had come his way.

At this camp, Pinkerton personally interviewed refugees, deserters, and ex-slaves, looking for valuable information about the Confederate military. Occasionally, he hired one of the newcomers as a spy.

"I had especially noticed the young man who had given his name as John Scobell," Pinkerton wrote after the Civil War ended. "He had a manly and intelligent bearing, and his straightforward answers to the many questions . . . at once impressed me very favorably."

Scobell told Pinkerton that he and his wife had been slaves in Mississippi. They had traveled with their owner, also named Scobell, to Richmond, the capital of the Confederacy, where their master had freed them. Scobell's wife found a job in Richmond. He wanted to escape to the North. Along the way, he'd paid attention to Confederate military units and noted the roads and streams in the region.

Pinkerton acted quickly. Scobell could read and write, rare for slaves, since it was forbidden for them to learn to do so in the South. Over the next two weeks, Pinkerton gave Scobell various assignments, eventually offering to hire him as a scout. Scobell and Pinkerton bonded on a deeper level as well. Both Pinkerton and Scobell's former owner were Scots. Scobell could even speak with a Scottish accent.

Before long, Scobell passed the Secret Service tests for loyalty and secrecy. He set out with Pinkerton's best operative, Timothy Webster, to test his ability to be a secret agent. The two left for Leonardstown,

Virginia, where Webster would contact Southerners who believed him to be a Confederate sympathizer. Scobell's mission was to move among the slaves and gather information about the rebels.

Near Leonardstown, the two men split up. Webster checked into a hotel managed by a loyal Confederate whom he knew from the past. Scobell found quarters in the African-American community.

At the hotel, Webster began swapping information with the manager, who thought Webster was a Southern spy. Suddenly, a tall, bearded man burst into the room. The stranger glanced at Webster, then asked to speak privately with the hotel manager. When the manager returned, he informed Webster that the stranger was a surgeon, a Union deserter who was on his way to Richmond to deliver important letters to the Confederate secretary of war. Could Webster help him?

"I'll do what I can," Webster replied.

The hotel manager made arrangements for Webster and the surgeon to take a boat to Richmond the next day. Webster needed to find Scobell; he had a mission for him.

"As I have a little time before dinner, I think I'll take a walk to give me an appetite," Webster told the hotel manager.

Webster kept watch to see if he was being

followed. Meeting Scobell on the street, they agreed that Scobell would come by the hotel, where Webster would point out the surgeon.

That afternoon the hotel manager introduced Webster to the surgeon and informed them of the plans for the boat to Richmond. Eventually, the doctor rose, and Webster accompanied him to the door. Webster noticed Scobell standing in the shadows a short distance away. Now Scobell knew who the surgeon was. Webster walked back inside and over to the hotel bar with the manager.

About an hour later, the door to the bar burst open. The doctor entered, a fearful sight. His clothes were torn and dirty; he looked shaken and pale.

What happened?

"I've been attacked and robbed!" said the doctor.

On his way home from the hotel, he had walked through a patch of woods. Someone had attacked him from behind, hitting him hard on the back of the head. When he awoke, only the secret letters to the secretary of war had been taken.

Webster and the hotel manager comforted the deserter. After they had dinner together, Webster went out for a stroll. Before long, Scobell appeared. When they reached the outskirts of town, Scobell produced the stolen letters. The ex-slave smiled. Scobell

told Webster that he had already made arrangements to forward the letters to Pinkerton if Webster
approved. Scobell knew an African-American who
could take the letters to Washington. Webster asked
to meet him.

They walked to a sagging building with boarded-
up windows. Walking to the door, Scobell gave a low
whistle, and the door opened. It was dark inside.
Webster heard the door close behind him, then heard
Scobell whistle. According to Pinkerton, who later
recounted the story, this is what happened next:

"Who comes?" asked an unknown voice.

"Friends of Uncle Abe!" replied Scobell.

"What do you desire?"

"Light and liberty!"

A trapdoor opened above them, and a rope ladder
fell down.

Scobell sent Webster up the ladder first. By now,
Webster realized that he had entered a meeting house
of the Loyal League, an organization that worked
secretly to promote the end of slavery. Not only was
Scobell a talented spy: he held membership in the
league, one of the most effective antislavery groups
in the South.

"The League operated as a secret society, with
grips, rituals, and a password—'Lincoln, Liberty,
Loyal League,'" wrote a later historian. "The 4 Ls —

meeting in church or school buildings — Loyal Leagues held joint social and political gatherings."

The only furniture in the room consisted of a barrel with an American flag draped over it and a packing box nearby, the seat for the Loyal League president, who sat surrounded by about forty men.

The group welcomed Webster and Scobell. The group's president offered to take the packet of letters to Allan Pinkerton in Washington. Webster agreed to the plan and sewed the packet and a letter into the lining of the president's coat.

Webster returned to the hotel, and Scobell made his way to the African-American section of town. The next day, Webster and the doctor, still cursing the loss of his documents, set out by boat for Richmond. Scobell remained in town, where he made friends and gathered information that might be useful to the North. The Loyal League president delivered the letters to Washington, where they aided the Union side.

Pinkerton's instinct to trust Scobell with a secret mission had proven correct—the former slave had more than exceeded expectations. Now Scobell set off on a new adventure, to walk to Dumfries, Virginia, to gather information on Confederate troop movements.

Even though Scobell had been freed by his owner, he still had to operate in a segregated environment where most African-Americans were slaves. Scobell faced many barriers just to move around. For example, if he traveled with another agent, it was okay to ride a horse. But if he traveled alone, riding a horse would call attention to him. The assumption was that he was a slave—why was a slave riding a horse alone?

So Scobell started walking to Dumfries. It didn't take long for him to begin thinking of a quicker way to make the fifty-mile trip. Perhaps he could take a boat part of the way. But whites might be suspicious, not expecting him to be a paying passenger. He figured out a plan.

Tired from the day's walk, he stopped near the Rappahannock River and spent the night. Before long, a packet boat, the *Virginia*, steamed up to the dock. This boat carried mail, packages, and some passengers. Scobell boarded the boat and politely requested to work for his passage as far as Fredericksburg, Virginia. The captain questioned him harshly.

"'You . . . rascal,'" Pinkerton quoted the captain, writing later about the episode. "'What do you want at Fredericksburg? Come now, no lies, or I'll throw you into the river!'"

Scobell respectfully replied that he had family he needed to see in Fredericksburg.

"Well, go below and tell the cook to put you to work!" the captain roared.

That night the boat anchored to wait for the rising tide. An elderly African-American who worked on the crew brought out a banjo, and the crew began singing songs, including "Way Down Upon the Suwannee River." Before long, Scobell's baritone voice arose, singing a Scottish ballad. When he finished the number, everyone wanted to know where he'd learned the song and acquired the Scottish accent. The boat captain, a Scot himself, had been moved by the ballad; tears trickled down his face.

"Look here, young man, I need an extra hand on this boat," he said warmly. "I'll give you forty dollars a month to work for me. . . . What do you say?"

Scobell gladly accepted, using his Scottish accent.

When Scobell awoke before dawn the next morning, he hurried out to help unload the cargo at Fredericksburg. The boat was scheduled to depart for its next destination the following day, so Scobell asked the captain for permission to go ashore for a while. The captain not only said yes; he gave him some spending money, reminding him that the boat would leave without him if he didn't return on time.

Scobell did not return. Instead, he made his way to Dumfries and spent the next ten days gathering information to take back to headquarters.

Scobell became known as a good actor, a highly

prized skill for a spy. As he moved from place to place, he sometimes worked as "a vender of delicacies through the [military] camps, a laborer on the earthworks at Manassas, or a cook at Centreville. [H]e made his way uninterruptedly until he obtained the desired information and successfully accomplished the object of his mission."

On other occasions, Scobell escorted agents on missions. In April 1862, he visited his wife in Richmond and received orders to accompany another agent, Carrie Lawton, back to Washington. The two rode by horseback. Lawton held a Confederate pass, and Scobell was assumed to be her servant. But when they stopped at an inn, Scobell became suspicious of a peddler. Scobell thought that the peddler's beard was fake and that he seemed too interested in Lawton.

Just to be sure, Scobell secretly trailed the peddler to a cabin outside of town. There he confirmed that the peddler was wearing a disguise. Scobell returned to the inn. He and Lawton quickly took off for their next stop, a place called Glendale, where they expected to meet Lawton's husband and a detachment of Union officers. They rode at night through a wooded area. For a time, all was well.

"I guess we will get through all right, notwithstanding our fears to the contrary," Lawton said, according to Pinkerton's later account of the trip.

Scobell feared the peddler might show up somehow.

"There's still time for trouble yet," he said. "Perhaps we'd better walk the horses a spell."

After walking a few miles to rest the horses, they resumed the ride. About five miles from their destination, they spotted a grove of trees ahead.

"Just the place for an ambush," Lawton remarked. "Draw your pistols, John, and be ready in case of attack."

Both carried guns and were excellent shots. Just as they left the woods, they spotted four men galloping toward them. If challenged, they decided to each shoot the person at their side. When the group came closer, they could see that two wore Confederate uniforms, while the others wore civilian clothes.

"That one on your side is the peddler!" Scobell shouted.

"Halt!" one of the Confederates yelled.

Two shots rang out, and two of the men tumbled from their saddles. The other two stopped to help their fallen companions. Scobell and Lawton galloped ahead.

"They'll never get us now!" Scobell exulted.

But when he looked back over his shoulder, he saw the other two horsemen in pursuit. Suddenly, his horse jerked and stumbled to the ground, depositing Scobell in a ditch.

"Go ahead!" he yelled to Lawton. "Save yourself."

She galloped on, and Scobell helped his horse stand up. He placed a gun over the saddle and waited until he could see the two men clearly in the light of the moon. He fired. One man shrieked and fell from his horse; the other turned and fled in the opposite direction.

Scobell reloaded his gun and got ready to mount his horse. Now he heard horses coming from the direction in which Lawton had traveled. There must be a dozen riders!

They burst into sight; fortunately they were Union cavalrymen. Lawton and her husband dashed ahead of them.

"John!" Lawton exclaimed. "Are you hurt?"

"No," Scobell replied, adding that one assailant had fled. They sent a party of soldiers after the fleeing man, buried the two who had died, and bandaged the wounded soldier. The peddler, one of the dead, was a rebel spy.

"Mr. and Mrs. Lawton and [Mr.] Scobell soon afterwards returned to Washington," Pinkerton wrote of the episode, "where they were allowed to rest themselves for a time before being again called upon."

Long after the Civil War, Pinkerton continued to write about Scobell's "remarkably gifted" spying. Without a doubt, John Scobell served as one of the most "cool-headed, vigilant" detectives on Pinkerton's talented staff.

Conspirator or Innocent?

Her tiny cell closed like a coffin around Mary Surratt. She had no relief from the stifling July heat. Guards watched her every movement. For days, workers had yelled and joked as they built a scaffold in the outer courtyard for her hanging. Now she could hear the excited chatter of the crowds who had come to watch the execution. Spectators swarmed outside the prison, hoping for a glimpse of the condemned prisoners.

Many years earlier, it was unthinkable that little Mary Jenkins, a much-loved child of a farming family in southern Maryland, could wind up with a noose around her neck. But this sad event came about in part because of the enormous difficulties women faced during the Civil War.

When seventeen-year-old Mary Jenkins agreed to marry John Surratt, he seemed like a desirable mate. Ten years older than his bride, John was well established in the area and had business plans that sounded promising. However, John had bad traits, too. Mary learned that her husband was physically abusive. He not only owned a tavern but also drank frequently. John took out his rages on his wife. A devout person, Mary busied herself with running their tavern and farm and serving in her church and community.

About a year after the Civil War began, John died, leaving Mary with three children. Because of her gender, Mary had been barred from making business decisions. But after her husband's death, she suddenly was expected to function in the commercial world. Mary discovered the shocking news that her husband was deeply in debt. Not only did she have to somehow make a living to support her family; she had to negotiate with banks and creditors to prevent them from taking the tavern and farm. Just as Mary previously had no power in her late husband's decisions, now she had little say in the actions of her sons, even when they put her life into danger.

* * *

Maryland was a slave state neighboring Washington, D.C., the U.S. capital. Once Virginia seceded from the Union, Washington leaders panicked: If Maryland also joined the South, Washington would be surrounded by Confederates. Union officials took action.

U.S. military troops poured into Maryland, and the state remained in the Union, at least officially. However, many Marylanders supported the Confederacy, and thousands signed up to be Confederate soldiers. By the time the Civil War broke out in 1861, John Surratt chose to secretly support the South. The local post office that he operated was an official U.S. post office; however, it also functioned as an underground Confederate post office where Southern agents could receive messages and instructions.

Isaac, the Surratts' older son, took off for Texas when the war started. Eventually, he joined the Confederacy. Their younger son, John, Jr., became a courier for the Confederate Secret Service. He carried messages throughout Maryland and Washington. Sometimes he traveled as far north as New York or Canada.

In 1862, a little more than a year after the Civil War began, John Surratt died, and soon creditors began demanding their money. Eventually, Mary decided to rent out the tavern and move her family to a small house they owned in Washington. One of the few acceptable positions for women at the time was to operate a boardinghouse, a place where people could rent rooms and eat their meals in a dining room. Mary was hardworking and determined—surely she could operate a boardinghouse and save her family and property; her grown daughter, Anna, would help her.

Mary and Anna moved to a brick house on H Street in Washington. The house was conveniently located for business travelers visiting the capital city. Mary rented the tavern back in her hometown to a former police officer named John Lloyd. She hoped that a former officer would know how to manage the bar and pay his rent. Unfortunately, things did not work out that way.

Mary's three children were young adults by the time she opened the boarding house. John, Jr. frequently stopped by on his secret Confederate courier visits to Washington, where many spies operated. Sometimes, he stayed in Washington hotels. But as the war continued and the Confederacy had less money to give him, John stayed at the boardinghouse more often. Occasionally, his associates stopped by the boardinghouse to see him.

By 1863, John met with a variety of spies and

conspirators plotting to undermine the Union government. One of those men, a popular young actor named John Wilkes Booth, had hatched a daring plan to kidnap President Lincoln. Booth knew John and frequently visited him at hotels and at the boardinghouse. Mary and Anna did not involve themselves in the relationships between John and the men who visited him. Anna and her mother went to Mass at a nearby church every day. When John was at the house, he often met upstairs with his guests so they could speak freely away from his mother and sister.

On August 9, 1864, Booth registered at a hotel in nearby Baltimore. There he invited two friends from childhood, Samuel B. Arnold and Michael O'Laughlin, to visit. Both men had served as Confederate soldiers but did not know each other. Booth spun a heroic tale of how they would kidnap President Lincoln and change the direction of the Civil War.

In October 1864, Booth set out on a trip to Canada, where he contacted Confederate agents George N. Sanders and Patrick C. Martin. Martin provided Booth with letters of introduction to Dr. Samuel A. Mudd and Dr. William Queen, physicians in southern Maryland. Martin accompanied Booth to the Ontario Bank, where he deposited money and exchanged $300 in gold. Next, Booth traveled back to Washington and checked into the expensive National Hotel.

Conspirator or Innocent?

The time had come to begin their kidnapping plan. The first step consisted of building a network of contacts. Once the kidnapping took place, the group needed other helpers to ensure that they could escape with their victim.

According to some accounts, Booth purchased handcuffs, pistols, knives, two Spencer repeating carbines (short rifles), a pair of French field glasses, and a buggy and harness. He told potential recruits "they would make an immense fortune" by participating in the kidnapping. Not only would the kidnapping of Lincoln result in their being seen as heroes in the South; they would get rich as well!

Arnold later testified about Booth's contact with John Surratt: "Met him next day. Went to breakfast together, he was always pressed with business with a man unknown and then only by name, John Surratt. Most of his time, Booth's time, was spent with him. We were left entirely in the dark." According to Arnold, the conspirators expected "Surratt and unknown [man] to be on the opposite side of the bridge to facilitate escape."

The kidnapping plot continued until March 17, 1865, when Booth signaled his fellow conspirators that Lincoln planned to attend a play at a military hospital. Booth gathered his group at a nearby restaurant, intending to waylay President Lincoln on his way home from the play. At some point, Booth went out to check and returned to say that Lincoln had changed his plans. The president had detoured to the National Hotel, where he participated in a military ceremony. Lincoln had escaped capture! This must have infuriated Booth, who himself lived at the National Hotel.

The Civil War finally was nearing an end, with the Union prevailing. On April 3, 1865, Richmond, the capital of the Confederacy, fell to Union troops. The night before, Jefferson Davis, the president of the Confederate States of America, escaped from Richmond on a train. On April 9, Union general Ulysses S. Grant and Confederate general Robert E. Lee met at Appomattox Court House, Virginia, and Lee surrendered his army. Booth's grandiose plan to kidnap the U.S. president and exchange him for thousands of Southern troops vanished with the news of surrender.

On April 11, Booth attended a speech outside the White House in which Lincoln supported voting rights for African-Americans. Such a thought enraged Booth, who now resolved to assassinate Lincoln.

Good Friday, April 14, 1865, began as an ordinary day in Washington. However, life for most in America would never be the same again. President Lincoln and his wife were slated to attend the play *Our American Cousin* at Ford's Theatre in the capital.

Across town, Mary Surratt occupied herself with the chores of running her boardinghouse. Her son John was away. Anna kept to her usual schedule, assisting her mother supervise the help and attending Mass at a nearby church. Early on the Friday morning of the assassination, Booth learned that Lincoln would be attending the theater that evening. Booth sprang into action.

On April 13, Booth had resolved in his diary to kill Lincoln, but he had no definite plan. Booth was an actor and knew Ford's Theatre well. He even received his mail there. Booth knew exactly which box Lincoln would occupy during the play.

Booth realized that Lincoln might change his schedule, as he had done on the day of the planned kidnapping. Booth predrilled a small hole in the door of the presidential box at the theater so he could peek inside to be sure that Lincoln was there. Booth also knew he needed a getaway horse, so he contacted a nearby livery to rent one and made arrangements to have someone hold the horse outside the theater for his escape.

Next he informed three of his conspirators, Lewis Powell (also known as Lewis Paine), David Herold, and George Atzerodt, that he had decided to kill Lincoln and General Grant that night. Booth also wanted two of the conspirators to assassinate Secretary of State William H. Seward and Vice President Andrew Johnson. The conspirators were astounded. Earlier, they had joined in a plot to kidnap President Lincoln, a scheme they thought would lead to glory because thousands of Confederate troops would be released in exchange for Lincoln. Now they were being asked to *assassinate* the president of the United States, the vice president, and the secretary of state.

Booth's persuasive skills took over. He convinced the men that killing Lincoln and the other high officials would result in political chaos. Booth insisted there was still a chance the Confederacy might rally. General Robert E. Lee had surrendered his army of 50,000 men, but there were other Confederate armies that had not yet given up. Once the Union administration fell into disarray, the Confederate armies could revive.

On the day of the assassination, Mary received a fateful letter, one that led to a series of events that would seal her fate. The letter came from Charles Calvert, one of the people to whom her late husband owed a lot of money. He demanded repayment. Mary began a frantic effort to repay Calvert before he seized her property.

Calvert had instructed Mary in his letter to

pressure a man who owed her the same amount that Calvert was demanding. Mary hurriedly wrote a letter to him. Meanwhile, Booth's assassination plans moved forward.

Even though the other conspirators were shocked at the idea of killing Lincoln, eventually they agreed to go along with the plan. Booth assigned Atzerodt to kill Vice President Johnson while Booth took care of Lincoln. Booth appointed Herold to guide Powell to Secretary of State Seward's house. Then the two were to leave Washington and join Booth in the escape. Atzerodt set out for the Kirkwood Hotel, where Johnson resided.

Atzerodt was still uncertain about the idea of killing Johnson. He decided first to go to a bar and have a drink. More drinks followed. An unsteady Atzerodt eventually left the hotel and tossed his knife away. He wandered about Washington and finally took a room at the Pennsylvania House Hotel and fell asleep.

Powell, a former Confederate soldier, had agreed to kill Secretary of State Seward. He and Herold reached Seward's house in the Lafayette Park area of Washington. On the night of Lincoln's assassination, Seward lay in bed recovering from a carriage accident. Powell developed a clever plan for his surprise attack.

While Herold waited nearby, Powell knocked on

the front door and informed the butler that he had brought medicine for Seward and needed to show him how to take it. Powell walked up two flights of stairs to Seward's third-floor bedroom. Seward's son Frederick appeared and questioned Powell, who drew a gun and shot at Frederick. Powell missed, so he beat Seward's son over the head with the gun until he collapsed.

By this time, Seward's daughter Fanny had come out of Seward's room, so now Powell knew where the secretary was. Powell ran inside and attacked Seward with a knife. Seward's neck brace made it difficult for Powell to deliver a neck blow, and Seward managed to roll off the bed and move out of reach. Fanny and other household members tried to hold Powell, but he fought them off and fled. Herold took off when Powell did not return.

Meanwhile, Booth's plan to assassinate Lincoln was proceeding mostly according to plan. General Grant, Vice President Johnson, and Mrs. Johnson had declined the Lincolns' theater invitation. Instead, Major Henry Rathbone and his fiancée accompanied the Lincolns and sat with them in the theater box. Booth had prepared himself well for the drama of his life. He knew the play the Lincolns would be watching, and he waited until a moment when laughter would ring out.

Conspirator or Innocent?

When the audience began to laugh, Booth entered the box and barred the prenotched door so it couldn't be opened from the hallway. Lincoln sat in a rocking chair, watching the actors. Booth shot the president in the back of the head with a derringer, a short-barreled pistol. Major Rathbone tried to stop Booth from escaping, but Booth stabbed him with the knife he'd intended to use to kill General Grant. Rathbone absorbed the blow on his arm and tried to prevent Booth from jumping over the sill of the box.

Booth was fast and leaped to the stage below, but he was off balance from Rathbone's attempt to halt him. Booth caught his boot spur in a flag decorating the box. He landed with a thud on the stage, breaking his left leg. Dramatic to the last, he called out *"Sic simper tyrannis!"* the Virginia state motto in Latin, which means, "Thus always to tyrants." Then he limped across the stage, out the door, and leaped onto the horse waiting outside. The deed was done.

A doctor was summoned, but Lincoln's wound was too severe to treat. Men carried the president, unconscious, across the street to a boardinghouse and placed him diagonally across a bed—he was too tall to lie vertically. Other members of his cabinet arrived, along with other doctors. At 7:22 A.M. on April 15, 1865, President Lincoln died. The people present knelt for a prayer, and then Secretary of War

Edwin M. Stanton stated, "Now he belongs to the ages."

Lincoln's murder enraged the North. The Civil War had drained the country for the past four years. More than 620,000 soldiers had died in the war, along with countless civilians. The North had won, but now their president lay dead. The Lincoln administration, especially Secretary of War Stanton, launched an all-out effort to capture the conspirators.

They didn't need to look far—Booth, the man who shot Lincoln, was known to have met frequently with John Surratt, a member of the Confederate Secret Service. They often met at the boarding-house of Surratt's mother, Mary. Word went out to arrest everyone connected to Booth and John Surratt.

Of all the conspirators, only Booth had actually carried out an assassination. Except for President Lincoln, everyone else on Booth's hit list survived. Atzerodt had not even tried to kill Vice President Johnson. Secretary of State Seward had been seriously wounded but survived. General Grant was not even in Washington. Booth's plan to change the course of the Civil War shattered with the failures of his accomplices. Booth had temporarily escaped but now had to hobble on a broken leg from one hiding spot to the next. His conspirators faced their own problems.

Herold had guided Powell to Secretary Seward's house but dashed away when he heard a commotion inside. Herold caught up with Booth in Maryland. Herold was unharmed, but now he was accompanying a man wanted by every police officer and soldier in the North.

Powell, after failing to kill Seward, bolted from Seward's house and tried to fit in with the foot traffic in Washington. But he didn't know his way back to his lodgings and quickly became lost.

Atzerodt slept through the night, drunk, in a hotel room. But the next day, news of Lincoln's death and the search for the conspirators screamed from every newspaper. John Surratt had been out of Washington for several weeks. He later said he was in Elmira, New York, when he found out about Lincoln's death. Understanding his danger, John fled first to Canada and then to England and Italy.

Secretary of War Stanton firmly believed the Confederate government was behind the assassination and wanted to pin the crime on the Confederacy. When Lincoln was shot, there was no doubt who the gunman was. John Wilkes Booth, the famous actor, had leaped onto the stage and proclaimed his "death to tyrants" line before fleeing. But no one knew at that time who else was involved. Booth was still at large, lurking someplace in Maryland or Virginia, possibly accompanied by other conspirators.

By approximately 2 A.M. on Saturday morning, April 15, detectives descended on the Surratt boardinghouse. They asked lots of questions, especially about John, who had been out of Washington since April 3.

By Sunday night, detectives besieged the Surratt house. There was still no sign of John, so the government pulled the net tighter, drawing in everyone who might have encountered the plotters. At this moment, Mary suffered a stroke of bad luck. With her living room filled with detectives, a knock was heard on the front door. When she opened it, there stood Lewis Powell, the conspirator who'd attempted to kill Secretary Seward.

Powell had wandered the city since the murder attempt and finally found the Surratt boardinghouse. He was poorly dressed, covered in mud, and carried a pickax. He claimed that Mary had hired him to dig a gutter. Mary shrieked, "No," and said she'd never seen the man before. She had bad eyesight. Powell, normally a good-looking, well-dressed man, hardly resembled himself in his disheveled state. The detectives recognized Powell and promptly arrested Mary, Powell, and the others who lived in the house.

Conspirator or Innocent?

Perhaps imprisonment would induce them to lead the authorities to John Surratt and a connection to the Confederate Secret Service.

Booth and Herold had fled to Mary's hometown, where they stopped at Surratt's tavern to pick up weapons and supplies. Booth stayed outside while Herold went inside to see Lloyd, the proprietor. According to Lloyd's later accounts, the injured Booth stayed outside on his horse while Herold went inside to retrieve items left there earlier. Lloyd had placed two carbines in a space between floors of the tavern. Herold obtained only one carbine because Booth was unable to manage one with his broken leg.

The two fugitives moved on to see Dr. Mudd, whom Booth had met earlier. Mudd set Booth's leg and placed it in a splint. Then he fashioned a pair of crutches for Booth. Afterward, Booth and Herold connected with several other Southern sympathizers. One hid them in a swamp for five days until they could cross the Potomac River. Eventually, the two stowed away in a barn. When federal soldiers caught up to them there on April 26, Herold gave up.

Booth refused to surrender, and the soldiers set fire to hay around the barn. A soldier shot Booth, who was dragged out and placed on the porch of a nearby house. Booth suffered in agony for a couple of hours. "Tell my mother I died for my country," he said before dying.

By this time, any certainty of tying the assassination to Jefferson Davis and the Confederacy was fading. John Surratt, with his connection to the Confederate Secret Service, had vanished. Booth had died without naming any other conspirators. Booth's conspirators appeared to be a crew of misfits assembled by an actor creating a performance rather than a vast political conspiracy.

The War Department turned to Mary Surratt and the conspirators who had been caught—their punishment would have to suffice. Before leaving the boardinghouse, Mary asked to kneel and pray. That would be the last time she would ever see her home.

Mary did not face a normal trial. She did not appear before a jury of her peers. She did not stand before a judge who presided over the examination of evidence and then sent the jury out to reach a verdict. Instead, she and the other conspirators faced a military tribunal, typically reserved for soldiers. Yet none of the conspirators was in the military.

There were political advantages for the government in choosing a military tribunal. The rules for trying someone were easier than the ones required in a civilian court of law. In the meantime, the U.S. government pursued every angle they could find to capture John Surratt. They tracked him to England, but he disappeared again. The government hoped that if his mother was charged and risked hanging, he would surrender.

When questioned in prison, the male prisoners spoke at length about their plans to initially kidnap the president; yet none of their trial testimony claimed that Mary knew about the kidnapping plan. In fact, they all maintained that Booth had decided to kill Lincoln only shortly before the assassination.

The government ordered eight people tried for conspiring to kill Lincoln, Vice President Johnson, Secretary of State Seward, and General Grant. The eight tried were David E. Herold, the man who guided Powell to Seward's home and then joined Booth and hid with him until they were captured; George A. Atzerodt, the man who had been instructed to kill Johnson, but who never made an attempt; Lewis Powell, the man who attempted to kill Seward; Mary Surratt; Michael O'Laughlin and Samuel B. Arnold, childhood friends of Booth; Samuel Spangler, whom Booth had asked to hold his horse outside the theater; and Dr. Samuel A. Mudd, who'd set Booth's broken leg after the assassination. John Surratt was nowhere to be found.

With Booth dead, and with no statements from the other conspirators that involved Mary, the prosecution turned to two witnesses for the state. The first was Louis Weichmann, a friend of John Surratt. Weichmann maintained that Mary would often talk alone with Booth whenever he came by the house when John Surratt was away. He also stated that Mary spent time alone with Booth on the day of the assassination.

The most damaging testimony against Mary came from John Lloyd, the man to whom she'd rented the tavern. He was in great danger of being tried and hanged as a conspirator. He had supplied a weapon, field glasses, and whiskey to Booth and Herold when they stopped by the tavern after the murder. Instead, the prosecution used him as a witness against Mary, Herold, and the other conspirators and did not try him. Lloyd stated that Mary had told him to "have the shooting irons ready" that night. Lloyd said that John Surratt told him how to hang the rifles in a secret space between the two floors. When the house was searched after the assassination, the remaining weapon fell, immediately implicating Lloyd. Therefore, Lloyd provided the testimony that sealed Mary's fate. In return for his testimony, he saved himself.

On June 28, 1865, when the tribunal returned a guilty verdict against Mary, she screamed and fell to the floor. Mary and three other defendants, Herold, Powell, and Atzerodt, were sentenced to death by public hanging. The tribunal attached an additional recommendation of mercy for Mary, requesting that her sentence be reduced to life imprisonment. The prosecutor, Joseph Holt, delayed taking the orders to President Johnson until the following Wednesday, July 5, because the president was ill. Supposedly, President Johnson asked Holt to summarize the verdicts and did not read the finding asking for life imprisonment for Surratt. Johnson signed the execution orders and ordered the hangings to take place two days later, on July 7.

Because a military tribunal had been used instead of a civilian court, the defendants could not appeal to the appeals court or the U.S. Supreme Court. They could appeal just to President Johnson. The other four defendants were convicted but received only prison sentences. However, they were not told that they would not hang. The government kept that secret from them until after the other four were hanged.

Once Mary was convicted, various people appealed to Johnson to reduce her sentence. Five members of the tribunal who sentenced her signed a petition recommending that she be imprisoned for life rather than hanged. In addition to the personal petitions, there were numerous official appeals that might have worked under other circumstances. Even the head of the prison where Mary stayed traveled to the White House to ask for clemency.

It was not to be. Shortly before 1:00 P.M. on Friday, July 7, 1865, Mary and the other three prisoners to be hanged—Powell, Altzerodt, and Herold—formed a procession. Mary walked out first, held up by two officers. Two priests walked with her.

Once the condemned arrived on the scaffold, Powell thanked his guards and restated a declaration that he'd made over and over: "Mrs. Surratt is innocent. She doesn't deserve to die with the rest of us!"

A general read the execution order while soldiers pinned the prisoners' arms behind them and tied their legs together. Then white sacks were placed over the heads of the condemned, and nooses were placed around their necks. General Winfield Hancock, in charge of the military district, clapped his hands twice, and soldiers knocked down the standing posts, which jerked the support posts down about five feet. The prisoners now hung above the crowd; Mary Surratt "swung and twirled—perfectly quiet," one account said. She apparently died instantly.

After the executions, Mary's son John left his hiding place in Canada. Former Confederate agents helped him to book passage to England. From there he went to Rome and served as a guard in Vatican City. The U.S. had offered a $25,000 reward for his return. An old friend recognized him and notified the U.S. ambassador. Surratt escaped and lived for a time in Italy, then booked passage to Egypt, where he was arrested in November 1866. He was sent home by ship, but the USS *Swatara* did not return to the U.S. until May 1869.

By the time of Surratt's return, the U.S. Supreme Court had determined that civilians could not be tried by military tribunals if civil courts were in operation. Therefore, John was tried in a civilian court in the District of Columbia instead of by a military tribunal as his mother had been. Surratt admitted his part in planning to kidnap Lincoln—which didn't happen— but denied any part in the assassination. After a two-month trial, John Surratt was released for a mistrial, in which eight jurors found him innocent, while four voted guilty.

Surratt became an upstanding citizen after his trial. He lectured publicly on the assassination trials. He taught school and eventually became treasurer of a steamship company. His older brother, Isaac, also worked with his brother's company. John Surratt married a descendant of Francis Scott Key, and they had seven children. He died in 1916 at age 72.

Anna Surratt was devastated after the death of her mother. For a time, her mother's attorney tried to pressure Anna to sell the family property so he would be paid. However, she could not legally sell the property without her brother John's signature, and he did not return for several years. Eventually, Anna moved to Baltimore to teach, and in June 1869, she married a former Union officer named William P. Tonry. He and Anna had four children.

The four additional conspirators who were *not* hanged were all sent to Fort Jefferson, a prison in the Dry Tortugas, a group of islands off Florida. Arnold, Mudd, and O'Laughlin received sentences of life imprisonment, and Spangler, the man Booth asked to hold his horse at the theater, received a six-year sentence. O'Laughlin died of yellow fever in prison. In 1869, President Andrew Johnson pardoned the other three prisoners.

Mary Surratt had not been allowed to speak at the military tribunal that convicted her. The last answer she gave in her statement to the man who questioned her in prison was a sad comment on her fate. Mary was asked if her son or Booth or Atzerodt "ever [told] you that they had engaged in a plot to kill the president?"

Conspirator or Innocent?

"Never in the world if it was the last word I have ever to utter," she replied.

Mary Surratt's trial took place at a time in history when many people on both sides of the Civil War were more interested in continuing the fight than in seeking justice. She was one more death in a long list of casualties in a tragic conflict, one that would continue for generations.

Confederate Spy

Volunteering for military service was surprisingly difficult for Frank Stringfellow. When the Civil War began in 1861, Southerners of all ages rushed to enlist in Confederate units. A skilled rider and an expert marksman, Frank's skills exceeded those of many recruits. Well educated, he had left a teaching job in Mississippi to return home to Virginia to sign up in a local unit.

First, he tried the Little Fork Rangers. They turned him down. Next, he thought he could enroll in the Madison County unit. No luck there. Then he set his sights on the Goochland County Dragoons, followed by the Prince William County unit. No, and no again. Many might have given up after four rejections. Instead, Frank Stringfellow switched gears. He went over to where the Powhatan Troop had camped, drew his gun on three guards, and marched them to the tent of the company commander. There he requested to join up, telling the officer he would capture Yankees next time. This time, Frank's approach worked. Eventually, he became one of the most famous Confederate spies of the war.

Why did the first four units reject the young recruit? For starters, he weighed only ninety-four pounds and was plagued by a persistent cough. Because of his delicate features, Frank didn't resemble the muscular, rough-and-ready soldiers depicted on the military posters of the day. However, as the commander of the Powhatan unit had discovered, Frank brought other advantages.

For starters, most people underestimated him. If one approach didn't work, he tried another and another. He never gave up. Even being captured proved to be no problem for Frank, who escaped many times. Friendly toward many of his enemies, they sometimes sheltered him, even when they knew he belonged to the opposite side. He led a charmed life as a spy.

Frank's unit operated under General J. E. B. Stuart, a famous Confederate general, who requested that Frank be his personal scout. One of his early assignments sent Frank to Alexandria, Virginia. Before the war, he had attended school in Alexandria, directly across the Potomac River from Washington. He still knew many people in the area, which gave him an advantage in spying. Frank's youthful looks earned him a job as an apprentice to a dentist. He had no dental skills, but apprentices usually started out as teenagers with no background in the field. He fit right in.

Frank's primary spying duty in Alexandria involved scanning the local newspapers and preparing a report on the material he'd read. Each night he placed his information in an envelope that he hid outside under the eaves of the roof. Someone—he never knew who—picked up the documents.

Stringfellow's identity was carefully disguised: His alias was Edward Delcher, a real-life Maryland dental assistant. The Union had sent many troops into Maryland to prevent it from seceding, but the state still harbored Southern sympathizers. Frank carried Edward Delcher's medical certificate from the Union, which said Delcher was unfit for military service—something people might believe about the skinny Frank. In fact, the real Edward Delcher actually served as a Confederate soldier down in Mississippi.

For seven or eight months, the assignment went

well. Then the unexpected happened. As Frank entered the dentist's waiting room, a young woman called out, "Frank!"

She was Emma Green, his longtime girlfriend, who had no idea he was back in town. She had accompanied her grandfather to the dentist's office. Even riskier than being identified, Frank saw another patient in the waiting room whom he suspected was a Pinkerton detective.

"No," Frank replied. His name was Delcher. He didn't know her at all. To her credit, she quickly apologized and asked no questions.

Soon another risk developed. The dentist's father-in-law was a Union officer. Frank had feared the dentist's wife might suspect his Confederate ties. She didn't know if Frank was a spy, and it didn't matter to her. She despaired of her husband's inattention and decided to start a rumor about Frank to make her husband jealous. She hinted to her husband that Frank was interested in her. That got her husband's attention, and it put Frank's life in danger.

One evening, the dentist's wife showed up at Frank's room and announced that her husband had gone to the Union authorities to betray him. Frank escaped out a back window and made his way to a friend's house where he had left a Confederate uniform. From there, he fled to Yorktown, Virginia, where General Stuart's troops waited.

After Frank's return to Stuart's unit, he learned that his mother had been wounded in the foot after her house had been taken over by Union troops. Stuart offered to send him on a mission near his mother's house. A member of Stuart's staff had written a book on Confederate general Stonewall Jackson, so Frank took an autographed copy along to give to his mother. He hadn't figured out yet how to get past the Union officers occupying her house—a small matter.

As Frank made his way toward his mother's home, he passed the camp of Union general Samuel Carter. A more cautious spy might have avoided the area, but not Frank. Instead, he sneaked into the encampment and located the general's unguarded tent. Frank crept inside and rummaged about until he found a captain's uniform, which he donned. He gathered up the papers on the general's table and took off. Federal troops shot at him, and he dropped the book. The Union troops thought they'd killed Frank, but he was unharmed and resumed his journey to his mother's home.

By the time he arrived, darkness had fallen. He slipped up to the house and looked through a window. It was filled with Union soldiers. A slave moved toward the window, carrying a lamp. Frank gently tapped the window, and the woman stared outside. Earlier, word had arrived that Frank had been killed, though no one had told his mother. The slave thought she saw a ghost! The lamp slipped from her hands, and the house caught on fire.

Frank slipped away into the darkness. Inside the house, Union soldiers doused the blaze. When Frank saw another slave, a man he knew as Uncle George, exit the back door and head for a spring carrying a bucket, he caught up with him, identified himself, and asked him to find some women's apparel. Once dressed as a woman, Frank managed to steal up to his mother's room.

Their reunion was interrupted by a doctor's visit. Frank hid in a closet. After the doctor treated Frank's mother's wound, he gave her the book her son had dropped in the Union camp and disclosed that Frank had been killed—though his body had not yet been found. Grieving, the mother said that she just couldn't believe her son was dead. Ever the spy, Frank made notes of the doctor's military comments on the closet walls, which still display the notations to this day.

Not only did he spend a few days with his mother; Frank managed to eat well while he lingered. One Union officer who commented on his stay at the house marveled how "one frail and wounded woman could eat so much."

Frank stole away from the house one night and made his way back to his headquarters. He carried intelligence about the Union troops staying at his mother's house, along with the papers pilfered from General Carter. The latter included a divisional payroll, which provided valuable information on the unit's troop strength.

In the early months of 1864, the Confederates in Frank's unit captured a Union captain. Among his papers lay a pass for a young woman named Sallie Marsden, who lived near Culpeper Court House. One of Marsden's brothers had been reported as missing, so she had crossed federal lines to look for him and had met the Union captain, who had acquired the pass in the hope Sallie would attend a dance with him. Now the captain was prison bound, and he asked Frank to take a letter to her. Frank knew the Marsden family.

Frank was happy to call on Sallie Marsden and deliver the captain's letter. While there, he borrowed a ball gown, hoops, and other female garments. He intended to impersonate Sallie at the George Washington Birthday Ball. Sallie and her mother carefully rehearsed Frank in proper etiquette for the ball. They also showed him how to add hair pieces to his hair so he could pin it up in a graceful style.

There was just one glitch in attending the ball: "Sallie" had no escort. The guard at the gate asked about the captain's name on the pass. Where was her escort? Delayed, fibbed "Sallie." He would meet her at the dance. The pass was genuine, so "Sallie" proceeded to the ball. Once inside, a steady stream of Union officers asked to accompany the beautifully dressed young "woman." Before long, a talkative major noted that General U. S. Grant would soon be redeployed as the Union general opposing Confederate general Robert E. Lee. This was valuable military information.

Still suspicious about having allowed an unescorted woman into the ball, the lieutenant who'd questioned "Sallie" suddenly appeared. He'd learned that the escort on the pass was a Union captain who had been reported captured. An unescorted woman at a military ball was a problem in another way; some might think she had a bad reputation. The lieutenant insisted that she leave. He personally would escort her home in a buggy—not a wise idea, as he would soon discover.

Leaving the dance, Frank whipped out the derringers (small pistols) he'd hidden in the trousers rolled up under his hoop skirt. Frank directed the officer to drive to the Confederate lines. Frank then produced his Confederate pass, and the Union lieutenant found himself a prisoner. According to one account of the journey, the lieutenant muttered, "My God, how did this ever happen to me?"

Benjamin Franklin Stringfellow

In May 1864, General Stuart, Frank's commander, was killed at Yellow Tavern, Virginia. Thereafter, Frank reported directly to General Robert E. Lee. His new role was to reconnoiter, or monitor, enemy troops before and during battles. Soon he received notice of a special assignment that came from the top of the Confederacy.

Lincoln had been reelected president in November 1864, another blow to the South. Lincoln's political opponent had been George B. McClellan, the Union general who had been relieved of duty in 1862. To many Southerners, any candidate was better than Lincoln. The war continued to lay waste to both sides, but conditions in the South were becoming desperate. In Richmond, the capital of the Confederacy, plots formed to try to reverse the direction of the war. The Confederate Secret Service grew ever more active.

"In secret sessions during February 1864, the Confederate Congress passed a bill that authorized a campaign of sabotage against the enemy's property by land or by sea," reported a later account of the Confederate Secret Service. "The bill established a Secret Service fund—$5 million in U.S. dollars—to finance the sabotage. As an incentive, the saboteurs would get rewards proportionate to the destruction they wreaked. One million [dollars] was specially earmarked for use by agents in Canada. . . . They believed that their plans for large-scale covert actions could win the war."

Among the plans being considered were:

- Schemes to kidnap President Lincoln and exchange him for Confederate prisoners
- Efforts to turn dissent into open rebellion in Northern states, such as Ohio, where many Southern sympathizers, called Copperheads, lived
- Plots to use newly devised torpedo bombs to destroy ships and federal property. Torpedo bombs were coal fragments that had been hollowed out and replaced with explosives. The rigged coal would be loaded aboard Union ships along with ordinary coal. When the torpedo bombs reached the fires in the ship's boilers, a gigantic explosion would take place.

Before Lincoln's inauguration in March 1865, Jefferson Davis, president of the Confederacy, dispatched Frank into Washington on a mission. The full extent of the assignment remains unknown to this day. Numerous Confederate agents had concocted plans to kidnap Lincoln and exchange him for vast numbers of Confederate prisoners or otherwise change the direction of the war.

Frank himself had created a kidnapping plan. During his stay in Washington, Frank stayed at several places, including the boardinghouse owned by Mary Surratt, the woman later hanged as a conspirator in the Lincoln assassination. He delivered at least one message to a foreign consulate, or official office of a foreign country. He also contacted high-ranking Union officers willing to sell information to the Confederates.

The Confederate leadership in Richmond did not seem to realize how quickly the war was drawing to a close. With General Lee's army starving and its troops often ragged and barefoot, the Confederate Secret Service still conducted numerous activities, convinced that the war could still be won.

By early April 1865, Frank learned that Richmond was being evacuated. He hurried to a livery stable to rent a horse but encountered a detective there who pestered him with questions. Word had spread that Frank, the Confederacy's most famous spy, was in the capital.

Frank contacted a source used by the Confederate Secret Service and acquired horses, a carriage, and a driver to make his escape. Frank and his driver were soon stopped by federal troops, who weren't satisfied with his papers. They insisted on taking him to their superiors.

Along the way, Frank secretly chewed and swallowed nearly all the papers he'd hidden in his pockets. But a report on Washington's defenses proved to be too bulky to eat. When he was searched, the soldiers discovered the report. They sent him to Port Tobacco, Maryland, where he was held for two days. On his second night there, he got up to get a drink of water and left the latch on the door ajar. Guards slept close by. Later that night, Frank escaped and ran for the woods. He used a trick he'd practiced before: He hid behind a log and covered himself with leaves. Being a thin man had its rewards. Soldiers combed the area for an hour and then moved on.

Meanwhile, John Wilkes Booth shot President Lincoln on April 14, 1865, and the president died the next day. Frank, traveling south on foot, reached Virginia after about three weeks. He found that he was suspected of being one of Booth's conspirators because his stay at Mary Surratt's boardinghouse had surfaced. Now he had a $10,000 reward on his head. He contacted Confederate operatives who lived in the area. They helped him escape to Ontario, Canada, by the summer of 1865.

From Canada, Frank wrote to his girlfriend, Emma. He stayed in Canada until after the Lincoln assassination trials took place. When Richmond finally fell to federal troops, Judah Benjamin, the Confederate secretary of state, ordered the Confederate Secret Service's files burned. Eventually, Frank accepted an amnesty offer from the U.S. government and returned to the U.S.

While in Canada, Frank had had time to mull over his deeds in the war. He wrote to Emma that his life was changing—that a "new life is opening up to me." After he returned to America, he entered the Episcopal Seminary of Virginia, was ordained, and became a priest. He and Emma married, and Frank served Episcopal congregations throughout Virginia.

Years later, when the Spanish-American War broke out in 1898, Frank again wanted to go to war, this time as a military chaplain. Again, he faced turndowns. The U.S. Army showed no interest in a fifty-seven-year-old, so Frank wrote to President William McKinley for assistance. He included a passage from a letter from President U. S. Grant.

During the Civil War, Frank had devised a plan to capture Grant, then the general in command of all the Union forces. Soon after the battle of Cold Harbor, Virginia, Frank sneaked behind enemy lines close enough to Grant to shoot him in the back. Frank had shot numerous soldiers in the war, but this time he hesitated. He just couldn't shoot someone in the back.

After the war ended, Frank wrote to President

Grant and related the episode. In turn, Grant thanked him and stated that he or a later president would be happy to honor a Frank Stringfellow request. President McKinley granted Frank's wish. Frank served in the Spanish-American War as a U.S. Army chaplain. This time, he ministered to American troops instead of spying on them. Once again, he returned home safely and continued his ministry. He died in 1913 and is buried, along with Emma, in the Ivy Hill Cemetery of Alexandria, Virginia.

In the Heart of the Confederacy

Elizabeth Van Lew lived at the top of Church Hill in Richmond, Virginia, the capital of the Confederacy. She occupied one of the fanciest houses in town, the place where some of the city's most important families came for dinner. Although Elizabeth had grown up in the South, she became one of the most important spies for the North.

She did so at high personal risk. Many Richmonders knew that Elizabeth had freed her slaves years before the Civil War, and that she supported abolition, the freeing of the slaves. Many Virginians suspected that Elizabeth might be disloyal to the South, so she had to watch her every move.

The Van Lew house was huge. It occupied an entire city block and looked out on landscaped gardens that sloped down to the James River. Sometimes Van Lew hid important Union prisoners in the house when they escaped from Confederate prisons. Often she hid them in a secret room. She didn't always tell the family members who lived with her (her mother, her brother, his wife, and their two children) what she was doing. There were many servants in the house as well.

One evening, Elizabeth seemed to be up to something. She had already eaten dinner, but she filled a plate with food and took it upstairs. Her young niece saw her and "followed her on tip toe to see what she was doing," a friend later wrote. "[S]he followed so quietly that Miss Van Lew, her aunt, never heard her." Elizabeth crept up to the attic.

"When her aunt opened the attic door, the little niece crept after her," Elizabeth's friend wrote. "The box was moved—the panel slid back and a man's head appeared. He looked haggard, and his hair and beard were shaggy. He was just about to cry out, but the little girl put her finger to her lips to warn him and then slid quietly away."

Elizabeth moved to another area of the house, and

her niece slipped back upstairs. The girl moved the box and called out to the man. He told her how to push the spring, and when she did, he put his head out and talked with her.

"My! What a spanking you would have got if your aunt had turned around," he said with a laugh.

Soon she shut him back inside and went off to bed. She later said she never went to the attic after that, nor did she tell her aunt about what she had discovered.

Virginia has a proud history, having been founded in 1607 at Jamestown, the first permanent English settlement in the New World. But along with settlement came slavery. White owners of tobacco plantations used slave labor. The state is called "the mother of presidents" because eight U.S. presidents were born there, including four of the first five presidents: George Washington, Thomas Jefferson, James Madison, and James Monroe. Both Washington and Jefferson spoke out against slavery, yet both owned slaves. Many important Civil War battles took place in Virginia, primarily because Union forces were always trying to occupy Richmond, the Confederacy's capital.

Elizabeth had grown up in a slave-holding family. Her father, John C. Van Lew, owned one of the major hardware companies in Richmond as well as a plantation outside the city. John Van Lew supported slavery and owned slaves that he used in his businesses and for household work.

Church Hill, the hill on which the Van Lew house stood, received its name from St. John's Episcopal Church, the place where Patrick Henry had given his "Give me liberty or give me death" speech during the Revolutionary War. Elizabeth, a church member, met many important Richmond families at church each week. Soon she would know a great many others—African-American and white, Northern and Southern—who participated in a wide-ranging spy network of her own making. Elizabeth, above all else, was a spy—a spy not for her native South but for the North.

Even as a child, Elizabeth had been known to think for herself. She didn't necessarily accept the opinions of her father, her minister, or her neighbors. Her parents had grown up in the North, and her mother sent her to a Quaker school in Philadelphia, where Elizabeth's grandfather had been mayor.

Quakers are known for their humanitarian activities and for rejecting war. Pennsylvania Quakers also regarded slavery as immoral. Elizabeth spoke out often against slavery, arguing heatedly with her father.

By 1808, importing slaves into the U.S. had been

outlawed. But selling slaves and their children still was allowed in many states. Richmond had one of the most important slave markets in the U.S., long before it became the capital of the Confederacy in 1861.

Elizabeth argued especially against the sale of family members of Van Lew slaves. Such debates sometimes took place at her family's dinner table.

Elizabeth was Southern, but she described herself as "a good Southerner who opposed slavery." To many Richmond whites, Elizabeth's opposition to slavery meant that she was not a "real" Southerner. In fact, a white who attacked slavery was considered to be treasonous, a serious offense. Whites who heard of Elizabeth's statements responded with anger, calling her a "willful little creature" and worse.

When her father died well before the Civil War began, Elizabeth and her mother freed their family's nine slaves, most of whom remained with the Van Lews and worked for pay. Elizabeth used her $10,000 inheritance to repurchase sold-off family members of their freed slaves. Such actions were deplored by most of her white neighbors, who never forgave her, even decades later.

Although Elizabeth antagonized most of the whites of Richmond, she still was connected to the community. Distinguished guests attended events at the Van Lew house for decades. Visitors included church bishops and the chief justice of the U.S. Supreme Court. Jenny Lind, the famous singer, performed in their parlor. Edgar Allan Poe read his poem "The Raven" aloud at a family gathering.

When the Civil War broke out between the North and South in April 1861, Elizabeth began to think about how she could aid the North.

Richmond held many Union soldiers in military prisons, where conditions were terrible. Confederate soldiers often suffered from lack of food and supplies; there was even less for Union prisoners. Elizabeth began to visit Union prisoners and supply food, books, and clothing—often from her own family. Secretly, she gathered information for the Union, particularly for General Ulysses S. Grant and his intelligence operation.

Elizabeth used many methods to acquire intelligence for the Union cause. Long before the war, she had aided African-Americans in Richmond. Former slaves were happy to join her spy network, sometimes carrying messages, supplies, or medicine.

One of the many good deeds that Elizabeth performed involved a family slave named Elizabeth Ann. After Elizabeth's father died, she freed Elizabeth Ann and others. Slaves often took their owner's last name, so this woman may have been called Elizabeth Ann Van Lew (or, after she later married a freed slave named William, or Wilson, Bowser, Elizabeth Bowser).

Elizabeth Ann was highly intelligent. After receiving her freedom, she continued to work for pay for the Van Lews. However, Elizabeth Van Lew had a new job in mind for this young woman: spy.

Elizabeth Van Lew created a new identity for Elizabeth Ann; she became Ellen Bond, a dimwitted, slightly crazy servant—a role similar to one often portrayed by Elizabeth herself as she moved around Richmond. Elizabeth arranged for Bond to assist someone she knew at a Confederate White House social event.

The Confederate president, Jefferson Davis, and his family were not originally from Richmond, so they did not know all the local gossip. They did know that the Van Lew family was wealthy and assumed that their servants had to be slaves. The Davises made another wrong assumption: that Bond couldn't read or write. In the South, teaching slaves to read or write was illegal. Bond was not only free and educated (Elizabeth had sent her to a school in Philadelphia before the war); she also possessed a photographic memory.

Now Bond had the opportunity of a lifetime: She

was working full-time for President Jefferson Davis. She served at dinner and listened intently to the Confederate officers speaking about their strategies and upcoming battles. When Bond cleaned Davis's office, she carefully read documents that she thought might be important. Next she contacted the Van Lew network and passed along the information she'd gathered, sometimes through a friendly baker.

Thomas McNiven, a respected local baker, delivered his fresh bread every morning to the Confederate White House. None of the Confederates suspected that McNiven was a spy, one of dozens in Van Lew's spy network. Bond often met McNiven at his wagon and chatted as she obtained bread for the day, providing any tidbits that needed to be forwarded to Elizabeth. As McNiven made his way around the city, he easily delivered bread—and information—to the Van Lew household.

Elizabeth constructed an elaborate system of conveying military information to Union generals. She set up five relay stations that extended from her Richmond house all the way to the headquarters of Union general George H. Sharpe, chief of the Bureau of Military Information. Her network included a variety of people, from former slaves and their family members to Union sympathizers not just in the community but even in the Confederate military.

* * *

When Van Lew received permission to visit Union prisoners, her reports to Union intelligence agencies greatly increased in value. Imprisoned officers provided more information than she'd ever been able to obtain before. Some inmates were able to peer out their prison windows to see nearby troop movements. As officers, they were able to estimate the strength of Confederate troops and supply trains and could often predict their destinations. They also reported scraps of conversations between surgeons or between guards—all of which would be reported to Elizabeth.

Elizabeth sent messages using a cipher, or secret code, system. She wrote her most important information in invisible ink. One of Van Lew's nieces wrote about the invisible ink many years later. The ink was colorless and was kept in a small bottle. When the receiver wanted to read the message, he or she simply added milk, which turned the ink black.

Some people who relayed messages were former slaves whom she had freed. One elderly man routinely slipped a coded paper in a hollowed sole of his shoe. He often made trips to the Van Lew farm outside Richmond. Frequently, he brought back food, such as a basket of eggs. One of the eggs would be hollowed out and a message inserted.

In the Heart of the Confederacy

* * *

One of the most feared Confederate prisons housed female prisoners. Called Castle Godwin, it held women suspected of disloyalty, spying, or harboring deserters. This prison gave Elizabeth and her mother nightmares about what could happen to them if their activities were discovered.

Numerous prisons existed in Richmond, but Libby Prison was visited the most by Van Lew because Union officers held there provided the most useful information. Libby consisted of three former tobacco warehouses. More than 50,000 men passed through Libby Prison. Many died from starvation, disease, and wounds that went untreated. Elizabeth's visits to Libby assured the prisoners that someone knew they were there and might get word to their families.

Running the Union's most important spy network, Elizabeth and her family lived in daily fear. If anyone surfaced who could prove that Elizabeth was a spy, she and her family members would have landed in one of the prisons or be hanged.

Another serious threat to Elizabeth's network was the group of men called White Caps. They operated outside the law and spread terror among people thought to be weak in their support of the Confederacy. The White Caps were an early version of what later became the Ku Klux Klan (KKK). The White Caps, like the KKK in later years, threatened residents, burned houses and buildings, and committed violence.

The White Caps often left threatening messages. One note found in Elizabeth's papers, now held in the archives of the New York Public Library, states:

> Old maid,
> Is your house insured? Put this in the fire, and mum's the word.
> Yours truly,
> White Caps

Another White Caps letter, accompanied by a skull and crossed bones, which signified death, said:

> "Look out for your fig bushes.
> There ain't much left of them now.
> White Caps are around town.
> They're coming at night.
> Look out!
> Look out!
> Look out!
> Your house is going out.
> Captain Fire
> White Caps

In spite of the threats, Elizabeth continued her

operations. She had many methods of getting information out of the prisons. A prisoner might whisper to her. Sometimes prisoners would leave notes in books. When she dropped off books, she also left a copy of her cipher. Later, when she picked up the books again, she might find letters lightly underlined. Then she would go back and put the words together. Instead of underlining, sometimes prisoners would put tiny holes under letters.

Sometimes questions and answers were concealed in baskets of food. She had an old French tray, a metal platter with a double bottom originally designed to hold hot water to keep the contents warm. Its frequent use aroused questions from a prison guard. Elizabeth was sensitive to what was going on around her and picked up on his suspicion. Several days later when she returned to the prison with the tray, a guard said, "I'll have to examine that."

"Take it, then," Elizabeth replied. She slipped off the shawl covering the tray, placing the tray in his hands. That day, the bottom contained no secret messages. Instead, it contained what it was supposed to hold: boiling water. The guard dropped the tray, gasping in pain.

Though often afraid, Elizabeth stayed focused on her goal: providing the best information possible to the North. As more Confederate citizens questioned her activities, she developed one new tactic after another.

Confederate soldiers had repeatedly searched the Van Lew home. Therefore, Elizabeth decided to offer the home to a new commandant at Libby Prison. The commandant and his family accepted her offer, so she had the Confederate prison chief comfortably living in her house, while she was busily feeding information to the Union through her network.

As the war went on, the loss of life on both sides was staggering. More American soldiers died in the Civil War than in all other U.S. wars combined. Approximately twice as many soldiers died of disease as of injury, particularly of dysentery, malaria, and typhoid.

In June 1864, about 50,000 Union soldiers attacked 30,000 defenders north of Richmond. Rifle and cannon fire cut down approximately 7,000 federal soldiers during the first three minutes of their attack. In the next month of fighting, General Grant lost almost 40,000 men. But the Confederacy also was suffering. After three years of war, Southern soldiers and civilians alike suffered from lack of food, medicine, and clothing. Thousands had been displaced by the war, their homes destroyed. Troops on both sides looted farms and cities. No civilian horse was safe.

Horses, like soldiers, fell in battle by the thousands.

In the Heart of the Confederacy

It was not unusual for a Richmond lady to be driving along in a carriage, only to be stopped by Confederate soldiers. Even though the woman supported the Confederacy, she would be left stranded with the buggy—and no horses.

For some time, Elizabeth had owned six magnificent horses, which she feared would be confiscated by the Confederates. To protect the horses, she hid them in her cellar. One day, Confederate officers appeared at her house and inquired about them.

"What horses?" she asked.

The officers said they'd need to search her house.

Elizabeth said that would be no problem and offered the men cake and liqueur. While the soldiers feasted in the dining room, Elizabeth sent one of her servants downstairs to move the horses. Then she instructed another servant to escort the soldiers to the basement—with the wrong set of keys! While they tried to find the right key, she spread straw on the dining room floor upstairs. Eventually, she dispatched the right keys, and while the officers searched the basement, she led the horses over the heavily carpeted floor into the dining room—where she now fed them cake to keep them quiet. The officers finally left, puzzled at not finding the horses but pleased with their cake and drinks.

*   *   *

General Sharpe, now chief of the Union Secret Service, wrote after the war, "The greater portion of our intelligence in 1864 and 1865 in its collection and, in good measure, in its transmission we owed to the intelligence and devotion of Miss Elizabeth Van Lew."

Elizabeth had backed the winning side in the Civil War, yet the postwar years were not easy for her. White Richmonders turned a cold shoulder to her for the rest of her life. Elizabeth had spent her family's fortune on the needy prisoners she had visited and to help the endless stream of people who came to her for aid.

After Van Lew's death in 1900, the niece who once had followed her up the stairs to the secret room returned to her aunt's house. "[The niece] who had been the little girl visited the old house and rediscovered the secret room; after more than forty years her fingers searched out and again pressed the hidden spring," according to a *Harper's Magazine* article on Elizabeth in 1911. "And then she told of that other time when she'd opened the door. . . . She has never forgotten what she saw as she peeped fearfully into the attic from the head of the stairs—the shadows and the ghostly shapes of the old furniture around the walls; her aunt, shading the candle with her hand, standing before a black hole in the wall, from which peered a haggard soldier . . . his thin hand outstretched for the food."

Just as Elizabeth's niece never forgot the episode with the hidden soldier, many of the people whom she fed, freed, and saved from harm never forgot, either.

At Elizabeth's grave site in a Richmond cemetery, a "great gray stone" is inscribed:

ELIZABETH L. VAN LEW
1818–1900

She risked everything that is dear to man —
friends, fortune, comfort, health, life itself,
all for the one absorbing desire of the heart —
that slavery might be abolished
and the Union preserved.

This Boulder from the Capitol Hill in Boston
is a tribute from Massachusetts friends.

Scout, Spy, Expedition Leader

By the time Harriet Tubman became a spy, she had already been a hero three times over. She had survived brutal treatment from a cruel slave master that left her maimed for life. She had led out of bondage more than 300 former slaves, transporting them from the South all the way to freedom in Canada. She had become known as Moses (the biblical figure who led his people out of slavery to freedom) among the newspapers of the North and among slaves and abolitionists. Yet the Civil War still raged, and most slaves still lived in bondage.

In 1862, she received a new type of call for help. Harriet was living comfortably in a small house in upstate New York. Her elderly parents, whom she'd rescued in a daring raid, lived with her, along with other former slaves she'd led to freedom. She farmed, tended a garden, and spoke to groups on abolition and women's rights.

This new call for help was unusual. She had been asked by the governor of Massachusetts to accompany a group of Massachusetts volunteer soldiers to South Carolina. The governor proposed an ambitious plan: Harriet would lead slaves away from their plantations and join the Union troops. This time Harriet wouldn't be operating alone as she had in the past. Now the U.S. Army would protect her. How could she refuse to help free others?

When Harriet landed in South Carolina in May 1862, she began two years of service with the military, and they achieved astonishing results. She put to use the medical knowledge she had gotten from other slaves, who knew how to coax medicine from roots, bark, and the buds of plants.

And she knew how to persevere, to keep on trying when others failed. She trusted her dreams and intuition—the *feelings* that she would have to beware or not trust someone. She had never learned to read or write; the laws in slave states forbade it. But she knew songs. From childhood, Harriet reached out to protect those she loved and friends and strangers who could not defend themselves. This expedition demanded every skill she possessed.

Once she arrived in Port Royal, South Carolina, Harriet began working with Dr. Henry K. Durant, the director of a hospital that treated former slaves. A variety of fevers and other serious illnesses plagued the ex-slaves and federal soldiers. All of Harriet's herbal skills were desperately needed. Yellow fever, typhoid fever, and typhus joined cholera, malaria, and dysentery to wreak havoc on troops and the local populace.

Miraculously, Tubman did not falter, even when she treated those with the dreaded smallpox. She, like the soldiers, had difficulty speaking with the former slaves, who spoke Gullah, an English–West African dialect.

Despite her efforts to help as many as she could, resentment among the former slaves built against Harriet over her handling of rations provided by the military. As more and more slaves left the plantations for protection by the U.S. soldiers, providing enough food became a serious problem. Some ex-slaves resented that Harriet received the same rations that soldiers did.

Hurt by their reaction, Harriet refused to accept

rations for herself. Instead, after long days of nursing people in need, she returned to her little cabin and built a fire. According to a biographer to whom Harriet later dictated stories of her life, "In this way she worked, day after day, till late at night; then she went home to her little cabin, and made about fifty pies, a great quantity of gingerbread, and two casks of root beer. These she would hire some contraband [a slave who had escaped to the Union lines] to sell for her through the camps, and thus she would provide her support for another day. . . ."

After nearly a year of nursing the ill, commanders in South Carolina ordered Harriet to organize a scouting force, the reason the governor of Massachusetts had sent her there. Harriet traveled freely in the area, but none of the local whites suspected her of being a spy.

By this time, two Union regiments of African-American soldiers had arrived, one led by Colonel Thomas Wentworth Higginson and the other by Colonel James Montgomery. Harriet knew Higginson and his mother personally. She shared a powerful connection with Montgomery, though she did not know him personally. Years earlier, Montgomery had supported John Brown, the controversial abolitionist who would later be hanged by federal troops for attacking a U.S. armory to begin a slave uprising.

Harriet, too, had backed Brown, though she was not with him when he attacked the armory. Now she served as the commander of her unit.

One of Harriet's greatest triumphs was the Combahee River Raid, which took place in South Carolina on June 2, 1863. The land in this area constituted some of the most valuable property in the Confederacy. Splendid plantation houses looked out on the river, tended by hundreds of slaves. Harriet and her band of scouts made their way through the area, contacting slaves and instructing them to be ready to desert their masters and join the federal troops.

They attacked in the middle of night. Harriet and her scouts waited near the entrance of the Combahee River. Three federal gunships plied their way upriver, loaded with 150 African-American soldiers led by Colonel Montgomery. Harriet and her advance men had scoped out the territory, determining where the Confederates had laid torpedoes, explosive underwater devices hidden to blow up enemy ships.

As the gunboats passed by in the dark night, slaves gathered at points along the river. Harriet and her scouts had instructed the slaves where to wait in the outgrowth and then alerted the boat captains where to the pick up the slaves.

No one who saw the scene could forget it. The

gunboats sent smaller boats out to the banks to pick up the slaves, who brought with them not just children, friends, and neighbors but also personal belongings, pigs, and chickens.

"I never saw such a sight," Tubman said. "Sometimes the women would come with twins hanging around their necks; it appears I never saw so many twins in my life; bags on their shoulders, baskets on their heads, and young ones tagging along behind, all loaded; pigs squealing, chickens screaming, young ones squealing."

The chaos, noise, and darkness created panic. Everyone tried to get into the boats at the same time; others would grip the boats, fearful they might be left behind. Colonel Montgomery, standing on the upper deck, yelled to Tubman: "Moses . . . give 'em a song!"

Harriet sang a song with an ending where the slaves would join in. At the end of a verse, the slaves threw up their hands and shouted, "Glory," giving the boat captains an opportunity to push off.

More than 750 slaves escaped onto the gunboats that night, a devastating loss of property and labor to the planters in the area. The gunboats also carried about 150 African-American soldiers, who occasionally left the boats and torched Confederate plantation houses and buildings along the way.

In the first news account of the attack, published by *The Commonwealth*, an antislavery publication in Boston, Harriet's identity was cloaked:

"Col. Montgomery and his gallant band of 300 black soldiers, under the guidance of a black woman, dashed into the enemy's country, struck a bold and effective blow, destroying millions of dollars' worth of commissary store, cotton, and lordly dwellings, and striking terror into the heart of rebeldom, brought off near 800 slaves and thousands of dollars worth of property, without losing a man or receiving a scratch."

A week later, another article in *The Commonwealth* identified the woman who led the expedition as Harriet Tubman. Her reputation soared nationally and internationally.

Back at Port Royal, Tubman now faced the overwhelming needs of the newly escaped slaves—not only the 750 who arrived on the gunboats, but also the steady stream of fleeing African-Americans who made their way to Union-held areas. An estate taken over by Union forces in Port Royal served as a refugee camp, but conditions there were not easy.

Crowding, lack of sanitation, and rampant illness multiplied the miseries that the freed slaves faced. The military issued rations for troops, but shortages afflicted the refugee camps. By this time the South faced hardships everywhere. Armies of both sides ranged over the countryside, taking food, cattle, and poultry. Slaves took the opportunity to escape slavery, yet all too often they faced hunger and separation from the community they knew.

By this time, Harriet had been in South Carolina for more than two years. Exposure to illness and the overwhelming workload began to take a toll. She received letters from home, telling her that her parents were failing. By the fall of 1863, Harriet's health began to weaken, and she asked to return home by May.

When Harriet returned to New York in the summer of 1864, she found her parents doing better, and she gradually recovered her own strength. She visited some of the groups that had sent donations to aid her efforts in South Carolina. Eventually, she went to Philadelphia, where the Sanitary Commission, the organization responsible for the care of the Union wounded, prevailed upon her to go to Fort Monroe, Virginia, where she worked until the war ended. When she returned home after the Civil War ended, she found a steady stream of people coming to her for help.

In October 1888, Harriet lost her husband, a Civil War veteran she had married some years earlier. In 1890, Congress passed a law that allowed widows of war veterans to receive a small $8-per-month pension. Tubman applied and finally received this well-deserved pension—not for her own courageous service, but a widow's pension for having been married to a soldier.

Now that she received a modest pension, Tubman turned to the final goal she wanted to achieve. She had long wanted to purchase a building for needy elderly African-Americans. There were few such facilities in the U.S. A building next door to her house became available in 1896. Tubman enlisted a local church, which helped her obtain a mortgage. Eventually, she donated the property to the church with the agreement that the building be maintained for elderly African-Americans in need.

By 1897, a petition drive was launched by prominent families all over New England and their political friends. They demanded a military pension for Harriet—$25 per month—the same that men received. Two years went by before the matter was resolved. Harriet Tubman, scout, spy, expedition leader, would *not* be issued a military pension. But because of "special circumstances," her widow's pension was raised to $20 per month.

The Harriet Tubman Home, the facility that she had long imagined, was dedicated on June 23, 1908. According to one writer, this "became the only charity outside New York City dedicated to the shelter and care of African-Americans in the state." By this time, Harriet was in her 80s and had outlived many family members and friends. She had accomplished most of the goals she had set for herself, and the home she envisioned for the poor would continue after her death.

Harriet Tubman died on March 10, 1913. While she never received official recognition for her military service, she was buried with military honors in the Fort Hill Cemetery in Auburn, New York. Booker T. Washington, the most famous African-American of his time, gave the eulogy. She had lived by the creeds she set for herself. She believed in her dreams. She persevered.

ACKNOWLEDGMENTS

I have been blessed with the support and assistance of numerous people while working on *Civil War Spies*. In particular, I would like to thank Linda Ferreira, formerly editorial director of Scholastic, for first mentioning the project to me. I especially want to thank Roy Wandelmaier, editorial director for Scholastic, for his assistance and patience.

The staff and faculty at Minnesota State University Moorhead have been unfailingly supportive. Dean David Crockett and Mark Strand, my department chair, provided ongoing encouragement. Deb Hval, the department's special assistant, has stepped in to assist on numerous occasions.

In addition, I would like to thank Terry Condon and George Holland for their help and hospitality in Washington, D.C.; I am especially indebted to the Library of Congress, the National Archives, and the

Acknowledgments

Surratt House Museum. The proprietor of the former Surratt boardinghouse, now the Wok and Roll restaurant in Washington, D.C., was especially helpful in providing a tour of the premises.

In New York City, I am grateful for the assistance of the staff of the New York Public Library and the Columbia University Archives; in particular, I appreciate the guidance of Mel Mencher, my longtime friend from Columbia University.

For my research on Sam Davis, I especially value the contributions of the Sam Davis House and Museum in Smyrna, Tennessee; staff members Anita Teague, Jane Clemons, and Meredith Lane Toporzyek were very helpful. In Pulaski, Tennessee, Donna Baker, the executive director of the Giles County Chamber of Commerce, provided contacts for the local Sam Davis Museum. I especially appreciate the expertise from local historians Dan Watson and George Newman; Dan Watson's CD of additional material on Sam Davis was particularly useful. Tim Turner, tourism coordinator for the Giles County Tourism Foundation, provided information about historical sites in the Pulaski area.

I would like to especially thank Brad Mooy and his staff at the Little Rock Literary Festival for inviting me to speak on my various books, including *Civil War Spies*. Additional area researchers who provided assistance include Rhonda Stewart, Charles Rogers, and Kaye Lundgren from the Arkansas Studies Institute at the Butler Center for Arkansas Research. Linda McDowell of the Arkansas History Commission found material on a variety of topics.

In Boise, Idaho, I am particularly indebted to the staff of the Boise Public Library and to the staff of the Albertsons Library at the Boise State University Library, especially to Dr. Associate Dean Peggy Cooper. Most of all, I thank Hildegarde Ayer, who provided me with the opportunity to examine and reflect on my research.

In addition, I would like to thank the friends who have cheered me on: Dr. Merry George; Kate Permenter; and Gretchen Rosenberg, who provided me with numerous possibilities for interviews; Julie and Ernie Van Metre; and Shirley and Jim Beck.

Most of all, I would like to thank my daughter, Leigh Wilson-Mattson, for her unfailing assistance and feedback.